LIFE'S
LITTLE BOOK
OF
BIG JEWISH
ADVICE

LIFE'S
LITTLE BOOK
OF
BIG JEWISH
ADVICE

Rabbi
Ronald H. Isaacs

KTAV PUBLISHING HOUSE, INC.

Library of Congress Cataloging-in-Publication Data

Isaacs, Ronald H.
  Life's little book of big Jewish advice / Ronald H.
  Isaacs.
    p. cm.
  ISBN 0-88125-835-0
  1. Judaism--Quotations, maxims, etc. 2. Proverbs,
  Jewish. I. Title
  BM43.I85 2004
  296.7--dc22

                                    2004003451

              Published by
      KTAV Publishing House, Inc.
         930 Newark Avenue
        Jersey City, NJ 07306
      Email: info@ktav.com
           www.ktav.com
          (201) 963-9524
         Fax (201) 963-0102

Contents

Even the wisest of kings need advice
(Meiri)

Introduction

It is said that a wise person hearkens to advice (Proverbs 11:41). Over the centuries the Bible and its personalities, rabbinic authorities, poets, writers and teachers have offered a plethora of advice on a wide range of timely topics. Whether they are biblical interpretations, ethical maxims, or popular sayings, the timeless wisdom offered in a variety of forms continues to be of great value today. Gathered in this little volume are more than 400 of these sayings, listed alphabetically by topic, on a variety of topics, all meant to instruct, inspire, guide, and offer advice. This practical advice is not only meant for Jewish people, but for all people who seek to expand their wisdom and live a better life.

If you will set some time aside each day to read, consider, and put into practice these wise sayings I believe your life will be enhanced. Always remember that the day is short, the work is great, and the reward is much. And if not now, when?

May the how-to practical advice in this book enrich your life and help to always keep you on the good path of life.

Rabbi Ron Isaacs

Do not be quick to anger, for anger lodges in the bosom of fools (Ecclesiastes 7:9)

Anger

1. An angry person is unfit to pray. (Nachman of Bratslav)

2. When a sage is angry, he is no longer a sage. (Talmud Pesachim 66a)

3. Never anger a heathen, a snake, or a student. (Talmud Pesachim 113a)

4. Observe people when they are angry, for it is then that their true nature is revealed. (Book of Mysticism)

5. A gentle answer turns away anger, but harsh words stir up wrath. (Proverbs 15:1)

At five years, one is ready to study Bible
(Pirkei Avot 5:24)

Ages to Celebrate: Milestones

1. At age 10, one is ready to study Mishneh. (Pirkei Avot 5:24)

2. At age 13, one is subject to responsibility of mitzvot. (Pirkei Avot 5:24)

3. At 15 one is prepared for the study of Talmud. (Pirkei Avot 5:24)

4. At age 20 one should look to the pursuit of a livelihood. (Pirkei Avot 5:24)

5. At 30 one is at the peak of one's strength. (Pirkei Avot 5:24)

6. At 40 one gains wisdom. (Pirkei Avot 5:24)

7. At 50 one is able to counsel. (Pirkei Avot 5:24)

8. At 60 old age creeps in. (Pirkei Avot 5:24)

9. At 70 one gains fullness of years. (Pirkei Avot 5:24)

10. At 80 one reaches the age of strength. (Pirkei Avot 5:24)

*The person with an unimpressive argument
rattles off many of them*

How to Argue

1. One strong point is worth many weak ones. (Talmud Yoma 85)

2. If you protest long enough that you are right, you are wrong. (Folk saying)

3. One who seeks the truth must listen to one's opponent. (Isaac Samuel Reggio, *Torah and Philosophy*)

4. When a debater's point is not impressive, he brings forth many arguments. (Jerusalem Talmud Berachot 2, 3)

5. Every argument that is for a heavenly cause will ultimately endure. (Pirkei Avot 5:17)

Charm is deceitful and beauty is vain
(Proverbs 31:30)

Advice on Beauty

1. Three things gratify a man: a beautiful home, a wife and beautiful clothes. (Talmud Berachot 57)

2. The beauty of man is in his wisdom, the wisdom of a woman is her beauty. (Bet HaMidrash)

3. Real beauty grasps us before we can grasp it. (Shimoni)

4. Do not look too long on the beauty that belongs to someone else. (Ecclesiastes)

*Those who consider a thing proved simply
because it is in print are fools*
(Maimonides,
Letter to Yemenite Jews)

Books

1. Whoever is capable of writing a book and does not is as if he has lost a child. (Nachman of Bratslav)
2. My pen is my harp and lyre; my library is my garden and my orchard. (Judah HaLevi)
3. A book should never be used as a missile, a shield, or an object for punishment. (Judah of Regensburg)
4. Books are not meant to be shelved, but to be studied. (Sefer Chassidim)

*Fifty productive men are better than
two hundred nonproductive ones*
(Jerusalem Talmud Peah, 8:8)

Business

1. False scales are an abomination to God, but a just balance is God's delight. (Proverbs 11:1)

2. Better a small profit at home than a large one abroad. (Talmud Pesachim 113a)

3. In business, everything depends on assistance from heaven. (Talmud Megillah 6b)

4. A person's drive for charity should be prompted by the desire to give charity. (Nachman of Bratslav)

One who stammers or who cannot pronounce letters or words correctly should not be appointed a cantor
(Code of Jewish Law)

Choosing a Good Cantor

1. A cantor must be of good character, free of sin and have a good reputation. (Code of Jewish Law, Orach Chayim 53:4)

2. A cantor should be humble, acceptable to people, and possess a pleasant voice.

3. A cantor should be accustomed to chanting biblical selections. (Code of Jewish Law, Orach Chayim 53:4)

What is mine is mine and what is yours is yours (Pirkei Avot 5:14)

Character Types in People

1. The ignorant person says: "What is mine is yours, and what is yours is mine." (Pirkei Avot 5:10)

2. The saintly person says: "What is mine is yours and what is yours is your own." (Pirkei Avot 5:10)

3. The wicked person says: "What is yours is mine and what is mine is my own." (Pirkei Avot 5:10)

Open your hand to your brother, to the poor and to the needy (Deuteronomy 15:9-11)

How to be Charitable

1. The more you give to *tzedakah*, the more your wealth will increase. (Midrash Proverbs 1)

2. Give charity with kindness and your reward will increase. (Talmud Sukkah 49b)

3. Giving charity secretly will make you greater than Moses. (Talmud Baba Batra 9b)

4. Even if you are a poor person living on charity, you should still give charity. (Talmud Gittin 7)

Eat less and dress better (Ibn Tibbon)

Clothing

1. A person's dignity accompanies one's dress. (Exodus Rabbah)

2. The person who does not respect clothes will not benefit from them. (Talmud Berachot 62a)

3. The dress of a wise person must be free of stains. He should not wear the apparel of princes to attract attention nor the clothing of the poor which incurs disrespect. (Maimonides, Mishneh Torah 5:7–13)

4. A seat will be given to you according to your clothing. (Megillat Starim)

It is a good thing to confess to God
(Psalm 92:2)

Confession

1. One who confesses will always have a share in the world to come. (Mishneh Sanhedrin 43)

2. One who confesses one's transgressions cannot be brought to judgment. (Zohar iv, 231a)

3. One who confesses and forsakes one's sins will obtain mercy. (Talmud Taanit 16a)

4. One who conceals one's transgressions and does not confess will never succeed. (Peskita Buber 159a)

With little or much, be content
(Ben Sira 29, 23)

Contentment

1. Who is rich? One who is happy with one's lot. (Pirkei Avot 4:1)

2. Be content with a peck of carobs from one Sabbath eve to another. (Talmud Berachot 17)

3. Eat onions and sit in the shade. (Talmud Pesachim 114)

4. The slave is free when he is content with his lot, and the freeman a serf when he asks for more than he needs. (i.e. never ask for more than you need) (Tachkemoni)

The critic must be like a grinding-stone — to grind and not to cut (Moshe ben Ezra)

How to Criticize

1. A person who criticizes another . . . should administer the criticism in private. (Maimonides, Laws Concerning moral dispositions and ethical conduct, chap. 6, sect. 7)

2. When criticizing another always speak to the offender gently and tenderly, and point out that you are speaking only for the wrongdoer's own good . . . (Maimonides, Laws Concerning moral dispositions and ethical conduct, chap. 6, sec. 7)

3. The test of democracy is freedom to criticize. (David Ben-Gurion)

4. One who winks makes trouble. One who openly criticizes makes peace. (Proverbs 16:7)

5. Include yourself in any criticism. (Nachman of Bratslav)

Do not whistle, since demons like this sound
(Russian folk saying)

Repelling Demons

1. Expectorate and use your saliva while saying "pooh pooh pooh." (Folk saying)

2. Close all books that are left open. (Folk saying)

3. Do not walk on thresholds, since demons often reside there. (Folk saying)

4. Placing salt in your home or in your pocket, will help eradicate demons. (Folk saying)

If one dreams that an ox has eaten of his flesh, one will become rich
(Talmud Berachot 56b)

Deciphering A Dream

1. If you see a donkey in a dream, you may hope for salvation. (Talmud Berachot 56b)

2. If you see white grapes in a dream, it is a good sign. (Talmud 56b)

3. If you see an elephant in your dream, a miracle will be created for you. (Talmud Berachot 56b)

4. If one sees wheat in a dream, you will see peace. If you see barley, your sins will depart. (Talmud Berachot 56b)

5. If you see little pomegranates in a dream, your business will be good. (Talmud Berachot 56b)

6. If you see a rooster in your dream, you may expect a male child. If you dream that you are going up on a roof, you will attain a high position. (Talmud Berachot 57a)

Ameliorating a Disturbing Dream
(Based on Talmud Berachot 55b)

1. (This verse is said 7 times) I have seen a good dream.

2. You have changed for me my lament into dancing. You undid my sackcloth and girded me with gladness. (Psalm 30:12)

3. God redeemed my soul in peace from the battles that were upon me, for the sake of the multitudes who were with me. (Psalm 55:19)

4. I create fruit of the lips. "Peace, peace, for the far and near," says God, and I shall heal him. (Isaiah 57:19)

5. (Recite this verse 3 times) God, I heard what you made me hear and I was frightened.

6. (Recite this verse 3 times) A song to the ascents. I raise my eyes to the mountains, from whence will come my help? My help is from God, Maker of heaven and earth. (Psalm 121:1–2)

7. May you reveal to me the path of life.

When you wage a war against a city . . .
do not destroy its trees (Deut. 20:19)

Ecological Advice

1. One should not be trained to be destructive. (Maimonides, *Mishneh Torah*, Laws of Mourning 14:24)

2. If one kills a tree before its time, it is like having murdered a person. (Nachman of Bratslav)

3. If you are setting up a tannery, be sure that the prevailing winds can send the odor away from the town. (Jerusalem Talmud Baba Batra 2:9)

4. Whoever breaks vessels, tears clothes, demolishes a building, stops up a fountain, or wastes food, in a destructive way, transgresses the law of "do not

destroy." (Maimonides, *Mishneh Torah,* Melachim 6:10)

An enemy is not hidden in adversity
(Ben Sirah, Ecclesiasticus 12:8)

Enemies

1. Every person's enemy is under one's own ribs. (Bachya ibn Pakuda, *Duties of the Heart*)

2. If two people claim your help and one is your enemy, help that one first. (Talmud Baba Metzia 32b)

3. The kisses of an enemy are deceitful. (Proverbs 27:6)

4. Who is a hero? One who can turn an enemy into one's friend. (Avot de Rabbi Natan, chap. 23)

Envy, cupidity, and ambition drive a person from the world (Pirkei Avot 4:28)

Envy

1. All types of hatred are curable except that which flows from envy. (Ibn Gabirol, *Choice of Pearls*)

2. No person can be called wise unless he possesses the quality of never envying someone richer than him. (Ibn Gabirol)

3. Envy is hatred without cure. (Bachya ben Asher, *Kad HaKemah*)

4. One who envies is guilty of robbery of thought. (Nachman of Bratslav)

5. The envy of scholars increases wisdom. (Talmud Baba Batra 21)

It is easier to abandon evil traits today than tomorrow (Chassidic Saying)

Evil

1. One who returns evil for good, evil will never depart from his house. (Proverbs 17:13)

2. Do not say, "I will repay evil." Wait for God to help you. (Proverbs 20:22)

3. The antidote to the evil impulse is Torah. (Talmud Kiddushin 30b)

4. Evil is sweet in the beginning, but bitter in the end. (Jerusalem Talmud Shabbat 14:3)

5. One who assists a fellow human being to do an evil thing is as if one had murdered that person. (Midrash Ha-Gadol 300

Never spread a costly garment over the bed
when guests are visiting your house
(Talmud Baba Metzia 30a)

Evil Eye (It's Prevention)

1. Put your right thumb in your left hand and your left thumb in your right hand and say: "I, so and so, son of so and so, am of the seed of Joseph, on whom the evil eye has no effect. (Talmud Berachot 55b)

2. Hang interesting objects (e.g. precious stones) between the eyes of the endangered person. (Tosef., Shabbat 4:5)

3. Qualify any praise that you give a beautiful object or person with the phrase "k'ayn ayin hara" [i.e. may there

be no evil eye) often shortened to "kay-nahora." (Jewish folk custom)

4. Never mention the date of your birthday or your exact age. (Jewish folk custom)

The righteous live by their faith
(Habbakuk 2:4)

Faith

1. A faithful person will be abundant in blessings. (Proverbs 28:20)

2. The exiles will be gathered in only at the price of faith. (Talmud Sotah 46)

3. There can be no faith without truth. (Zohar 3)

4. Faith is the foundation of all holiness. (Nachman of Bratslav)

5. In the struggle with evil, only faith matters. (Baal Shem Tov)

Flattery is permissible only to promote peace
(The Koretser Rabbi)

Flattery

1. Flattery leads to vulgarity, and the flatterer is despised. (Nachman of Bratslav)

2. A husband may flatter his wife for the sake of peace, his creditor to get attention, and his teacher to get special attention. (Otzar Midrashim)

3. A lying tongue brings destruction, and a flattering mouth works its own ruin. (Proverbs 26:28)

4. One who knows his friend to be wicked, yet flatters him, deserves all the imprecations in the Torah. (Yalkut Shimoni)

Miracles do occur, but they rarely provide food (Talmud Shabbat 53b)

Food

1. Food is better than drink up to age forty. After forty, drink is better. (Talmud Shabbat 152a)

2. If you have a fine meal, always enjoy it in good light. (Talmud Yomah 74b)

3. Always feed your pets before you sit down to eat food. (Talmud Berachot 40a)

4. Eat sparingly and lengthen your days. (The Koretser Rabbi)

5. One should eat slowly, properly, even if one eats alone. (Nachman of Bratslav)

Fools hate knowledge (Proverbs 1:22)

Fool Identification

1. The complacency of fools is their undoing. (Proverbs 1:32)

2. A fool will be a servant to the wise. (Proverbs 11:29)

3. The fool believes everything he/she hears. (Proverbs 14:15)

4. A fool is one who says in his heart "there is no God". (Psalm 14:1)

5. A fool is unable to feel an insult. (Talmud Shabbat 13)

Do not make friends with a person who is given to anger (Proverbs 22:24)

Making Friends

1. Let the honor of your friend be as dear to you as your own. (Pirkei Avot 2:5)

2. Always participate in your friend's joy on the day of your friend's success. (Ecclesiastes Rabbah 7)

3. Do not give your love to a friend all at once. (Ibn Gabirol, *Choice of Pearls*)

4. Never judge your friend until you put yourself in your friend's position. (Pirkei Avot 2:5)

Serve God with gladness (Psalm 100:1)

Feeling God's Presence

1. Walk in the ways of God. As God is merciful, gracious, righteous, and justice, so be you as well. (Sifre Ekev 85a)

2. It is according to one's deeds that God's Presence descends. (Midrash Eliahu Rabbah 8)

3. To love and feel God completely, you must first love human beings. (Chassidic saying)

4. When two people meet and exchange words of Torah, God's Presence (i.e. the Shechinah) hovers over them. (Pirkei Avot 3:3)

A good guest says: "Blessed is my host"
(Jerusalem Talmud, Berachot 9:1)

Good Guests

1. For a guest to bring another guest is considered bad manners. (Talmud Derech Eretz Zuta 8)

2. You will always be honored as a guest if you, too, can play the host. (Chaim Weizmann)

3. Do not come as a guest empty-handed. (Kurdish Proverb)

4. A courteous guest always says: All that my host labored to do, my host did for me alone. (Talmud Berachot 58)

Safety lies in the counsel of multitudes
(Proverbs 24:6)

Government

1. Where there is no vision, the people perish. (Proverbs 29:18)

2. Pray for political stability, for if not for the fear of the government people would swallow each other alive. (Pirkei Avot 3:1)

3. What kind of person is fit to govern? Either a sage given power or a king who seeks wisdom. (Ibn Gabirol)

4. A government can collapse because of one single injustice. (Chafetz Chayim)

It is advisable that a person should become accustomed to having breakfast in the morning (Abridged Code of Jewish Law, chap. 32)

Staying Healthy

1. More people die from overeating than from undernourishment. (Talmud Shabbat 22)

2. Anyone who sits around idly and takes no exercise will be subject to physical discomforts and failing strength. (Abridged Code of Jewish Law, chap. 31)

3. Asparagus is good both for the heart and the eyes. (Talmud Berachot 51a)

4. Sleep is like food and medicine to the sick. (Pirkei de Rabbi Eliezer)

5. Try not to eat meat unless you have a special appetite for it. (Talmud Chullin 84a)

Worship God in the beauty of holiness
(Psalm 29:1)

Holiness

1. In holy matters, we may promote but not demote. (Talmud Shabbat 21b)

2. There are sparks of holiness in everything. (Mezeritzer Rabbi)

3. If you eat in holiness and taste food in holiness, then your table becomes your altar. (Martin Buber)

4. The Holy Spirit rests only in a heart that rejoices. (Jerusalem Talmud, Sukkah 5:1)

Do not begin business on the new moon, on Friday, or on the Sabbath evening
(Sifra, Kedoshim 6)

Horoscopes, Lucky and Unlucky Days

1. It is dangerous to drink water on Wednesday and Friday evening. (Talmud Pesachim 112a)

2. There is danger in undergoing an operation on a Wednesday falling on the 4th, the 14th, or the 24th of the month, or on a Wednesday occurring within less than four days of the new moon. (Talmud Shabbat 129b)

3. People born on Sunday will be distinguished, on Monday, wrathful, on Tuesday, wealthy and sensual, on Wednesday intelligent and enlightened, on Thursday benevolent, on Friday

pious. Those born on Saturday are destined to die on that day. (Horoscope of Joshua ben Levi)

4. Those born while the sun rules in the heavens will have a brilliant career. Those born under the dominion of Venus are destined to wealth and sensual enjoyment. Those born under the planet Mercury forecasts intelligence and enlightenment. Those born under the moon's reign will suffer sorrow. The plans of those born under Saturn's reign will be destroyed, while righteous and giving people are born under Jupiter's reign. The shedder of blood is under the influence of Mars. (Talmud Shabbat 156a)

Be happy as you sit at your table and the
hungry are enjoying your hospitality
(Talmud Derech Eretz Zutah 9)

Good Hosting

1. Never watch your guest too attentively, as this will cause embarrassment. (*Mishneh Torah*, Laws of Blessings 7:6)

2. Rabban Gamliel, the Nasi [head of the Sanhedrin] served the guests at his son's wedding. [From this we learn that hosts should honor their guests by serving them personally] (Talmud Kiddushin 32b)

3. Let your home be wide open and the needy be members of your household. (Pirkei Avot, 1,5)

4. One who lodges a scholar in one's home is as one offering first fruits in the Temple. (Leviticus Rabbah 34:13)

A good wife who can find, her worth is far above rubies (Proverbs 31:10)

Husbands and Wives

1. A good wife is a crown to her husband. (Proverbs 12:4)

2. A silent wife is a gift of God. (Ben Sira 26,16)

3. A pleasant home, a pleasant wife, and pleasant furnishings enlarge a man's mind. (Talmud Berachot 57)

4. A man who takes a wife for the sake of money will have unworthy kids. (Talmud Kiddushin 70a)

5. A man who wants to take a wife should inquire about her brothers . . . (Talmud Baba Batra 110a)

A hypocrite will never see God's face
(Talmud Sotah 42a)

Hypocrisy

1. Four classes of people cannot see the Holy Spirit: mockers, hypocrites, slanderers, and liars. (Midrash, Psalms 101:7)

2. An idolater worships one object, but there is no limit to the number of people whom the hypocrite will worship. (Bachya ibn Pakuda, *Duties of the Heart*)

3. Hypocrisy is the tax which lie pays to truth. (Paphirna)

4. Beware the person who has two faces and two hearts. (Moses ibn Ezra)

*One who does not work will suffer
all of one's life* (Maimonides)

Idleness

1. Idleness leads to boredom. (Talmud Ketubot 58)

2. Idleness is a ladder for Satan and his helpers. (Maimonides, *Mishneh Torah*, De'ot 4)

3. One who is idle never has leisure. (Yiddish folk saying)

4. A person dies of idleness and boredom. (Avot de Rabbi Natan, 11)

An ignoramus cannot be saintly
(Pirkei Avot 2:5)

Identifying an Ignorant Person

1. An ignorant person is one who is exempt from an act yet performs it. (Jerusalem Talmud Shabbat 1)

2. For the ignorant, old age is winter. For the wise, old age is the harvest season. (Chassidic saying)

3. The ignorant think less clearly as they grow older. (Talmud Kinnim 3)

All Jews are responsible for one another
(Talmud Shevuot 39)

How to be a Jew

1. All Jews are brothers and sisters to each other. (Tanchuma Naso)

2. When a Jew sins, all Jewish people suffer. (Leviticus Rabbah 4,6)

3. It is difficult to be a Jew. (Shalom Aleichem)

4. Make the study of Torah your primary occupation. (Pirkei Avot 1:15)

5. A true Jew is distinguished by three characteristics: sympathy, modesty, and benevolence. (Pirkei Avot 5:22)

Joy finds its completion in success
(Immanuel of Rome)

Joy

1. A person's greatest joy is when one's family is with him. (Rabbi Ephraim Luntshitz)

2. God is with the joyous person while God forsakes the sad person. (Nachman of Bratslav)

3. Eat your bread with joy and drink your wine with a joyous heart. (Ecclesiastes 9:7)

4. Tears may linger at night but joy always comes with the dawn. (Psalm 30:6)

A fool raises his voice when he laughs, but
a wise person smiles quietly
(Ben Sirah, Ecclesiasticus 21:20)

Laughter

1. A person should fill one's mouth only with laughter in this world. (Talmud Berachot 30b)
2. Even in laughter the heart can still ache. (Proverbs 14:13)
3. It is a good sign for a person to die laughing. (Talmud Ketubot 103)
4. Weep before God and laugh before people. (Yiddish folk saying)

A leader must never think that God chose him for his greatness (Mendl of Kotzk)

Leadership

1. Try your best to control your passion and emotions. (Pirkei Avot 4:1)

2. Guide with humility, and you will lead people all the way into the World-to-Come. (Talmud Sanhedrin 92a)

3. Do not be arrogant for any reason. (Talmud Pesachim 113b)

4. Be able to take abuse with a smile. (Bratzlaver Rebbe)

5. Try to turn your enemy into your friend. (Avot de Rabbi Natan, chap. 23)

One who lends is greater than one who gives alms (Talmud Shabbat 63a)

Loans

1. One who makes a loan without stipulating the time of repayment should not ask for it until thirty days have passed. (Talmud Makkot 3)

2. Lending money without interest is more worthy than giving charity. (Talmud Shabbat 63)

3. Never lend money to another without witnesses. If you do, you have violated the law "place not a stumbling block [temptation] before the blind." (Leviticus 19:14)

4. One who does not lend money on interest, either Jew or Gentile, walks with great honor. (Talmud Makkot 24a)

Love is the greatest pleasure open to man
(Seder de Rabbi Eliahu Rabbah)

Love

1. A cheerful face makes for love. (Orchot Tzaddikim)

2. A fool's love is but a transient whim. (Rabbenu Tam)

3. One who is truly in love with another can read that person's thoughts. (Koretser Rabbi)

4. Love turns one person into two, and two persons into one. (Isaac Abravanel)

5. One who loves without jealousy does not truly love. (Zohar iii, 245)

Weep for the person who does not know his good luck (Talmud Sanhedrin 103a)

Luck

1. Two together are always luckier than one. (Talmud Baba Metzia 105)

2. Change your place and you will change your luck. (Talmud Shabbat 156)

3. If you do not rely on luck you will postpone misfortune. (Talmud Berachot 64a)

4. Work will change your luck. (Chayim N. Bialik)

5. Throw a lucky person into the sea and that person will come up with a pearl in his hand. (Ladino folk saying)

Saying the phrase "your ointments yield a sweet fragrance, your name is like finest oil. Therefore, do maidens love you" will arouse your love (Sefer Gematriot)

Magical Verses

1. Saying "the Lord bless you and protect you, may God deal kindly and graciously with you, bestowing favor upon you and granting you peace" [Numbers 6:24–26] will help drive away evil spirits. (Sefer Gematriot)

2. To gain a good name, say "you are fair my darling, you are fair with your dove-like eyes" [Song of Songs 6:4–9] (Sefer Gematriot)

3. To win credibility in an argument, say: "Give ear, O heavens, let me speak. Let the earth hear the words that I

utter. May my speech come down as rain, my speech distill as the dew, like showers on young growth, like droplets on the grass" [Deut. 32:1–2]. (Sefer Gematriot)

4. For a melodious voice, say "then Moses and the Israelites sang this song to God. I will sing to God, for God has triumphed gloriously. Horse and driver God has thrown into the sea" [Exodus 15:1]. (Sefer Gematriot)

If you have sons, wed them while young
(Ben Sira 7:23)

Marriage Advice

1. If a man and woman are worthy, the Divine Presence is with them. (Talmud Sotah 17)

2. One who marries one's daughter to a boor is as one that fetters her and throws her to a lion. (Talmud Pesachim 49)

3. No one may sanctify a woman for marriage before he sees her. (Talmud Kiddushin 41)

4. Marriages are made in heaven. (Genesis Rabbah 68)

5. When the betrothal is brief, the marriage lasts a long time. (Alcalay)

Radishes are good for fever
(Talmud Avodah Zarah 28b)

Medical Advice

1. How do you cure fever? Drink a small pitcher of water on the first day. (Talmud Gittin 67b)

2. If you have a nosebleed, call a Jewish priest whose name is Levi and write "Levi" backward. (Talmud Gittin 69a)

3. What do you do with a sore throat? Lubricate it with oil. (Talmud Berachot 36)

4. If you are constipated, eating dates will act as a laxative. (Talmud Gittin 70a)

Memory is the constant generator of history, human and divine
(Rabbi Nachum Schulman)

Memory

1. Remembrance brings action in its train. (Talmud Menachot 13)

2. One who listens to the rabbis and remembers their words is like a Rabbi himself. (Talmud Berachot 47)

3. Who is a sage? One who remembers one's learning. (Sifre Deuteronomy 1, 13)

4. The memory of the righteous is a blessing. (Proverbs 10:7)

5. In remembering is the secret of redemption. (Nachman of Bratslav)

Do what is right and good in the sight of God (Deuteronomy 16:18)

Menschlachkeit

1. Always vigorously pursue justice. (Deuteronomy 16:20)
2. Be a holy person. (Leviticus 19:2)
3. See peace and pursue it. (Psalm 34:15)
4. Be your brother's keeper. (Genesis 4:9)
5. Be just, kind, and walk humbly with God. (Micah 6:8)

*The son of David will not come until all
of the arrogant cease out of Israel.*
(Talmud Sanhedrin 98a)

Bringing the Messiah

1. The son of David will not arrive until the generation that will be either all righteous or all wicked. (Talmud Sanhedrin 98a)

2. The son of David will not come until all qualities are equal in all human beings. (Talmud Sanhedrin 98a)

3. The son of David will not come until there are no conceited people in Israel. (Talmud Sanhedrin 98a)

Do not depend on a miracle
(Talmud Pesachim 64b)

Miracles

1. Every favor which God performs for you is a miracle. (Zohar iv, 200b)

2. Miracles do not take place on the hour. (Talmud Megillah 7b)

3. There are only two ways to live your life. One is as though nothing is a miracle. The other is as though everything is. (Albert Einstein)

4. Believe in God through faith, and not because of miracles. (Nachman of Bratzlav)

Even birds recognize those who are ungenerous (Talmud Sotah 38)

Recognizing a Miser

1. A miser is like a mouse which lies on coins. (Talmud Sanhedrin 29)
2. Wealthy people frequently behave in a miserly fashion. (Talmud Menachot 86)
3. Miserliness is an expensive habit. (Chafetz Chayim)
4. The greatest miser with money is the biggest spendthrift with desires. (Moses ben Ezra, *Shirat Yisrael*)

A person is respected according to the manner in which one performs positive commandments in fear and love
(Tikkune Zohar)

Performing a *Mitzvah*

1. It is good to spend an extra third to perform a *mitzvah* in a more satisfactory manner. (Talmud Baba Kamma 9a)

2. The more *mitzvot*, the more well being for the body. (Avot de Rabbi Natan, chap. 28)

3. Who does not sin is rewarded as if one had performed a *mitzvah*. (Talmud Kiddushin 39)

4. If a *mitzvah* comes your way, do not delay. (Mechilta Bo)

5. One who performs a *mitzvah* extends the boundaries of heaven. (Zohar iii, 113a)

Run to perform even a light mitzvah
(Pirkei Avot 4:2)

Mitzvot

1. The performance of one precept draws the performance of another to its train. (Pirkei Avot 4:2)

2. The reward of a good deed is another good deed. (Pirkei Avot 4:2)

3. *Mitzvot* were given so that we may live by them. (Tosefta Shabbat 16)

4. It is well to spend an extra third to perform a *mitzvah* in a more satisfactory manner. (Talmud Baba Kamma 9)

When pride comes, so does scorn.
With the modest comes wisdom
(Proverbs 11:2)

Humility and Modesty

1. Modesty is the noblest of all ornaments. (Eleazar Rokeach)

2. God is a friend to the one who is humble. (Zohar ii, 233b)

3. My lowliness is my exaltedness. (Exodus Rabbah 45, 5)

4. Even if you are perfect in all of your virtues, you are imperfect if you do not have humility. (Kallah Rabbati 3)

A reputation is preferable to alot of wealth, and grace is better than silver or gold
(Proverbs 22:1)

Money

1. Whoever marries a woman for her money will have unworthy children. (Talmud Kiddushin 70a)

2. Perform charity and good deeds with your wealth, lest you fail to do them when you are without money. (Tanchuma Buber, Re'eh 7)

3. Respect other people's money as much as you do your own. (Pirkei Avot 2:17)

4. If you want to acquire wisdom, study the way money works . . . (Talmud Baba Batra 175b)

Go forth and see which is the good way to which a person should cleave
(Pirkei Avot 2:13)

Moral Conduct

1. Have an eye that looks favorably and with kind feeling. (Pirkei Avot 2:13)

2. Be a good companion and always extend a helping hand. (Pirkei Avot 2:13)

3. Be a good friend to your neighbor. (Pirkei Avot 2:13)

4. Have a good heart toward your fellow human beings. (Pirkei Avot 2:13)

Eulogizers who are untruthful are requited
(Talmud Berachot 62a)

How to Comfort Mourners

1. Do not speak to the bereaved until the mourner begins the conversation. (Talmud Moed Katan 28b)

2. Do not appease your fellow human being in the hour of his or her anger. (Pirkei Avot 4:23)

3. Silence is meritorious in a house of mourning. (Talmud Berachot 6b)

4. Never be joyful among the mourners. (Mishle Agur)

A flattering mouth works havoc
(Proverbs 16:28)

The Mouth

1. If you guard your mouth you will preserve your life. (Proverbs 13:3)

2. A fool's mouth is his ruin and his lips are a snare to himself. (Proverbs 18:7)

3. Make a door and a bolt to your mouth. (Ben Sirah 28:25)

4. The mouth, the hand, and the foot are under one's own control. (Genesis Rabbah 60)

As his name, so is the person
(I Samuel 15:25)

Names

1. A good name is preferable to riches. (Proverbs 22:1)

2. One who glorifies one's own name loses it. (Pirkei Avot 1,13)

3. A fair name is better than precious balm. (Ecclesiastes 1:7)

4. Win a good name and you may go to sleep peacefully. (Ladino saying)

5. There are three crowns: the crown of Torah, the crown of priesthood, and the crown of royalty, but the crown of a good name excels them all. (Pirkei Avot 4:17)

Love your neighbor as yourself
(Leviticus 18:19)

Neighbors

1. Shun a bad neighbor. (Pirkei Avot 1:7)

2. What is the good way whereto a person should strive to cleave? A good neighbor. (Pirkei Avot 2:9)

3. A bad neighbor counts his fellow's income, not his costs. (Deuteronomy Rabbah 9)

4. Never enter a neighbor's home unwarned. (Talmud Derech Eretz Rabbah)

Do not dishonor the old. We shall all be
numbered among them
(Ben Sirah, Ecclesiasticus 8:6)

Old Age

1. To honor an old person one should not sit in that person's place nor contradict that person's words.

2. The prosperity of a country is related to how it treats the elderly. (Nachman of Bratslav)

3. You shall rise before the aged and show deference to them. (Leviticus 19:32)

4. Long experience is the crown of the aged. (Ben Sirah 25:6)

5. Even in old age they shall bear forth fruit, they shall be full of vigor and strength. (Psalm 92:15)

Sneezing is a good sign (Folk belief)

Deciphering Omens

1. If your sole of your foot itches, you will soon be journeying to a strange place. (Chochmat HaNefesh 25d)

2. A howling dog is a sign that the angel of death is in town.

3. It is a bad omen to begin one's day or week with an action involving a loss. (Thus it is undesirable to pay the tax-collector on the first day of the week)

4. If you wish to engage in business and want to ascertain whether or not you will succeed, raise a cock. If it grows handsome and plump, you will succeed. (Talmud Horayot 12a)

5. An eclipse of the sun is a bad omen for the entire world.

As the mother, so her daughter
(Ezekiel 16:44)

Parenting Advice

1. Train a child in the way he should go, and even when he is old, he will not depart from it. (Proverbs 22:6)

2. Discipline your family to the simple needs of life. (Talmud Chullin 84a)

3. A child . . . should be pushed aside with the left hand and drawn closer with the right. (Talmud Sotah 47a)

4. Do not promise a child something and then not give it, because in that way a child learns to lie. (Talmud Sukkah 46b)

5. A man should never single out one child over another . . . (Talmud Shabbat 10b)

When passion burns within you, remember that it was given to you for good purposes
(Chassidic saying)

Passion

1. The pursuit of passion becomes boring. (Chassidic saying)

2. Our passions are like travellers. At first they make a brief stay, then they are like guests who visit often. Finally, they turn into tyrants, holding us in their power. (Talmud Sukkah 52b)

3. Who is a strong person? One who can control one's passions. (Pirkei Avot 4:1)

Whoever is slow to anger has great understanding (Proverbs 14:29)

Virtues of Patience

1. A person shows intelligence by his or her patience. (Proverbs 19:11)

2. A ruler may be won over using patience. (Proverbs 25:16)

3. Patience is the halfway mark toward knowledge. (Ladino folk saying)

4. A patient person is able to still contention. (Proverbs 15:18)

A doctor may not accept a fee for giving advice to a patient (Code of Jewish Law, Yoreh Deah, chap. 336, sec. 2)

Physicians

1. A doctor who charges nothing is worth nothing. (Talmud Baba Kamma 85a)

2. Doctors should make it their special concern to visit and treat the poor and the needy. (Isaac Israel, *Doctor's Guide*, no. 30)

3. A doctor should select attendants and caretakers who are capable of cheering up a patient. (Maimonides, *The Preservation of Youth*)

4. If your time has not come, even the doctor will not succeed in killing you. (Yiddish saying)

5. It is forbidden to dwell in a town without a doctor. (Talmud Sanhedrin)

Peace is important, for God's name is Shalom (Midrash Exodus 9)

Peace

1. The Holy Scripture was given to humankind in order to establish peace. (Midrash Tanchuma Yitro)

2. The world rests on three things: on justice, truth, and peace. (Perek HaShalom)

3. If there is justice, there is truth, and if there is truth, there is peace. (Perek HaShalom)

4. When there is no peace, prayers cannot be heard. (Nachman of Bratslav)

5. Wherever peace reigns, you need no courts. (Tosefta Sanhedrin)

There is no such thing as perfection
(Folk saying)

Perfection

1. The perfect human has a man's strength and a woman's compassion. (Zohar)

2. Humans are capable of perfection because of the power of reasoning that God gave them. (Maimonides, *Guide to the Perplexed*, I, 2)

3. A faultless person is possible only in a world without faults. (Hasdai, *Ben HaMelech vehaNazir*)

4. To be the acme of perfection is a fault. (Yiddish saying)

*Those who in their dreams see the Book of
Psalms may hope to gain piety*
(Talmud Berachot 57b)

Piety

1. Without wisdom there is no piety,
and without piety there is no wisdom.
(Pirkei Avot 3:21)

2. Beware of the pious ones who are
fools. (Ibn Gabirol, *Choice of Pearls*)

3. I am constantly afraid that I may
become too wise to remain pious.
(Koretser Rabbi)

4. The only truly pious person is the
indulgent one. (Sefer Chassidim)

Constant pleasure is no pleasure
(Chassidic folk saying)

Pleasure

1. One who pursues pleasure cannot control one's life. (Samuel HaNagid)

2. When one faces one's Maker, one will have to account for those Divinely given pleasures which one failed to enjoy. (Jerusalem Talmud, Kiddushin)

3. One that loves pleasure shall be a poor man. (Proverbs 21:17)

4. There are no pleasures without grief. (Eibshutz)

5. Pleasures are manifestations of God's name. (Baal Shem Tov)

*Wise persons who are poor are all too often
ignored* (Ecclesiastes 9:16)

Poverty

1. Poverty was created to give the rich an opportunity to give charity. (Anav, *Maalot ha Middot*)

2. In all labor there is profit, but mere talk leads only to poverty. (Proverbs 14:23)

3. Poverty makes handsome women ugly. (Talmud Nedarim 66b)

4. A poor person, if content, is rich. (Samuel HaNagid)

Prayer is the service of the heart
(Talmud Taanit 2:1)

Prayer

1. One who prays for one's neighbor will be heard for himself. (Talmud Baba Kamma 92b)

2. The prayer of a person who is ill is more effective than anyone else's, and is answered first. (Rashi)

3. One who prays without knowing what one prays does not pray. (Maimon ben Joseph, *Letter of Consolation*)

4. Prayers from the heart open all the doors of heaven. (Nachman of Bratslav)

5. One should not pray in levity and jest, but in gravity and the joy of doing good. (Talmud Berachot 31)

Wherever you go, I will go . . . (Ruth 1:16)

Proselytes

1. Dearer to God than all of the Israelites who stood at Mount Sinai is the proselyte. (Tanchuma Lech Lecha)

2. A proselyte who embraces Judaism is like a newborn child. (Talmud Yevamot 48b)

3. Proselytes are beloved, for in each and every passage the Bible likens them to Israel. (Numbers Rabbah 8:2)

4. Proselytes who study the Torah count as much as a High Priest. (Tanchuma Vayakhel)

Turn it (i.e. the Torah) over and over
(Pirkei Avot 5:24)

Qualifications
for Learning Torah

Here are 48 pieces of advice regarding qualifications for learning Torah:

Study, attentive listening, distinctive speech, understanding of the heart, awe, reverence, humility, cheerfulness, purity, attendance on the sages, associating with fellow students, close argument with disciples, sedateness, knowledge of Bible and Mishnah, moderation in business, worldly occupation, pleasure, sleep, conversation, jesting, long suffering, having a good heart, faith in the Sages, submission to sorrows, recognizing one's place, rejoicing in one's lot, making a fence around one's words, by claiming no merit for oneself, by being beloved, by loving God, by loving humankind, by loving well-being, by loving rectitude and reproof, by shunning honor and not boasting of one's learning, not delighting in making decisions, helping his fellow to bear his yoke and judging him favorably, directing him to truth and peace, being composed in study, by asking and answering, hearing and adding to it, learning in order to teach and practice, by making one's teacher wiser, retelling exactly what one had learned, and reporting a thing in the name of the person who said it. (Pirkei Avot 6:6)

Asking questions is a person's finest quality
(Solomon ibn Gabirol)

Questions

1. The fool wonders, while the wise person asks. (Benjamin Disraeli)

2. We are encompassed by questions to which only awe can respond. (Leo Baeck)

3. If one does not know how to ask, ask for him. (Passover Haggadah)

4. When you are asked a question and do not know what to answer, do not be ashamed to say, "I do not know!" (*Mivchar Hapeninim*)

Where God is blasphemed, no respect is due to the Rabbi (Talmud Berachot 19)

Rabbis

1. It is pious followers who make the Rabbi. (Mendel of Kotzk)

2. The Rabbi is just the person who knows the Torah, not the Torah itself. (Rav Tza'ir)

3. A rabbi whose community does not disagree with him is not really a rabbi, and a rabbi who fears his community is not really a man. (Israel Salanter)

4. Unless you know something about baseball, you will never get to be a rabbi in America. (Solomon Schechter)

*In your town, it is your name that counts.
In another, it is your clothes*
(Talmud Shabbat 145)

Reputation

1. Tombstones do not need to be erected on the graves of righteous people, for their deeds are their monuments. (Talmud Pesachim 119a)

2. Beauty diminishes, but a good name endures. (Apocrypha: Ahikar 2:49)

3. A good name is more desirable than great riches, a good reputation more than silver or gold. (Proverbs 22:1)

4. A place becomes known far and wide because it is the home of a great person. (Ropshitzer Rabbi)

*The righteous shall flourish like a palm tree,
and grow mighty like a cedar in Lebanon*
(Psalm 92:13)

Righteousness

1. Better a little bit of righteousness than great revenues with injustice. (Proverbs 16:8)

2. A righteous person cares for his animals. (Proverbs 12:10)

3. The mouth of a righteous person is a fountain of wisdom. (Proverbs 10:11)

4. There is not a righteous person upon this earth who does good and does not make mistakes. (Ecclesiastes 7:15)

It is a sign between Me and the children of Israel forever (Exodus 31:17)

The Sabbath

1. The Sabbath was given for the study of Torah. (Peskita Rabbati, 22)

2. The savior of the Jewish people is the Sabbath. (Falasha saying)

3. The Sabbath is a Queen whose arrival changes the humblest home into a palace. (Talmud Shabbat 119a)

4. One who takes delight in the Sabbath receives one's heart's desires. (Talmud Shabbat 118)

5. The most important ingredient in creating a Jewish home is the celebration of the Sabbath. (Abraham Joshua Heschel)

Let a person throw himself into a blazing furnace rather than shame a fellow human in public (Talmud Berachot 43b)

Shame

1. A person who has no shame will not inherit the world to come. (Zohar Chadash to Song of Songs, 67b)

2. It is better that you should be shamed through yourself than through others. (Talmud Derech Eretz Zutah 12b)

3. Do not shame and you will not be shamed. (Talmud Moed Katan 9)

4. It is better to delay a *mitzvah* than to bring shame upon anyone. (Talmud Sanhedrin 11)

5. Shame is an iron fence against sin. (Orchot Tzadikim)

Visit the sick and lighten their suffering
(Rabbi Eliezer ben Yitzchak,
Orchot Chayim)

Visiting the Sick

1. When visiting the sick, pray for them and leave. (Rabbi Eliezer ben Yitzchak)

2. Never stay too long when visiting the sick, and always enter the room cheerfully. (Rabbi Eliezer ben Yitzchak)

3. An enemy should not visit his enemy during his illness, for the sick person might think that his enemy rejoices in his misfortune. (Code of Jewish Law, chap. 193, sec. 1)

4. Relatives and close friends should visit the ill as soon as he/she becomes

sick. Others should visit after the first three days of illness. (Jerusalem Talmud, Peah 3:7)

5. When Rabbi Judah visited the sick, he would say, "May the Almighty have compassion upon you and upon the sick of Israel." (Talmud Shabbat 12b)

For many afflictions there is no better remedy than silence
(Talmud Megillah 18a)

Silence

1. Press your lips together. Never be in a hurry to answer. (Talmud Avodah Zarah 35a)

2. Silence protects wisdom. (Pirkei Avot 3:19)

3. A person was given two ears and one tongue, so that one may listen more than speak. (Hasdai, *Ben HaMelech vehaNazir*)

4. Unless you speak wisely, keep silent! (Immanuel of Rome)

One who secretly sins thrusts away God's Presence (Talmud Kiddushin 31a)

Sin

1. If a person has not sinned during most of his or her life, that person will not sin. (Talmud Yoma 38)

2. Remember these three things and you will not be led to sin: the all-seeing Eye, the all-hearing Ear, and the Recording Hand. (Pirkei Avot 2:1)

3. A sin hardens a person's heart. (Talmud Yoma 38)

4. The world's greatest sin is repeating anything without doing it in a new way. (Nachman of Bratslav)

5. The beginning of a sin is sweet and its end is bitter. (Ecclesiastes Rabbah 3:4)

One who slanders piles up offenses as high as the sky and deserves to be stoned
(Talmud Arachin 15)

Slander

1. Greater is the sin of the evil tongue than the sin of idolatry. (Midrash Gadul u'Gedolah, 18)

2. One who slanders, listens to slander, and who testifies falsely deserves to be thrown to the dogs. (Talmud Pesachim 118)

3. Speech that criticizes others even when they are not at fault embraces the evils of falsehood and slander. (Jonah ben Abraham Gerondi)

4. Who is the one who desires life, and loves many days, that he may see good? Keep your tongue from speaking evil,

and your lips from speaking deceit.
(Psalm 34:13)

Drowsing will clothe a person in tatters
(Proverbs 23:21)

Sleep

1. Sweet is the sleep of the working person. (Ecclesiastes 5:11)

2. Sleeping is one sixtieth of death. (Talmud Berachot 57b)

3. A rich person's wealth does not let him sleep. (Ecclesiastes 5:11)

4. Slumber is the first step to failure. (Genesis Rabbah 17:6)

My soul was also on Mount Sinai
(Exodus Rabbah 28:4)

The Soul

1. The soul is God's candle. (Proverbs 20:27)

2. Know that God is pure, and that the soul that God gave you is pure. (Talmud Niddah 30)

3. The soul is composed of three parts: power of life, power of endurance and power of higher feeling. (Zohar i. 81a)

4. When the soul is at peace, so will be the body. (Arama)

*Build your home in such a way that a
stranger may feel happy in your midst*
(Theodor Herzl)

How to Treat a Stranger

1. There shall be one law for the citizen and for the stranger who dwells among you. (Exodus 12:49)
2. Let your home be wide open and the needy be members of your household. (Pirkei Avot 1, 5)
3. You shall not wrong or oppress a stranger, for you were strangers in the Land of Egypt. (Exodus 22:20)
4. One who has fed strangers may have fed angels [as Abraham did].

*The student who pays respect to his teacher,
it is as if he were paying respect to God*
(Talmud Eruvin 5:1)

How to be a Good Student

1. Always live in the same town as your teacher. (Talmud Berachot 8a)

2. Do not contend against your teacher's ruling, for if you do, it is as if you contended with the Divine Presence. (Talmud Sanhedrin 110a)

3. Be quick to understand and slow to forget. (Pirkei Avot, 5:14)

4. Study out of love, and honor will come at the end. (Talmud Nedarim 62)

*If you see a person upon whom success
smiles do not forsake that person*
(Talmud Berachot 7)

Success

1. One who keeps on knocking will succeed. (Ben Ezra)

2. Success at times will kiss your lips, then recoil in rage. (Shlomo Rubin)

3. The real success is the success of the soul. (Albo)

Not to know suffering means not to be a man (Genesis Rabbah 92)

Suffering

1. If you want to live in this world, equip yourself with a heart that can endure suffering. (Leviticus Rabbah 30)

2. One cannot understand either the suffering of the righteous nor the prosperity of the wicked. (Pirkei Avot 4:21)

3. One day's happiness makes us forget suffering, and one day's suffering makes us forget all our past happiness. (Ben Sirah, Ecclesiasticus, 11:25)

4. A lack of accomplishment is the greatest suffering. (Chafetz Chayim)

*Do not become angry with your student
if he/she does not understand you*
(Code of Jewish Law,
Yoreh Deah 246:10)

How to be a Good Teacher

1. Always study and teach that part of
the Torah (i.e. subject matter) to which
your student is drawn. (Talmud
Avodah Zarah 19a)

2. Let the honor of your student be as
dear to you as your own. (Pirkei Avot
4:12)

3. Be a God-fearing person and possess the qualifications to teach accurately. (Code of Jewish Law, Yoreh
Deah 245:17)

4. With both your inner and outer self,
be consistent! (Talmud Yoma 72b)

Open your teaching with jest, and let your hearers laugh a little
(Talmud Shabbat 30b)

How-to Advice for the Teacher

1. If there are more than 25 children in an elementary class, appoint an assistant. (Talmud Baba Batra 21a)

2. To teach that which is in error is a transgression. (Pirkei Avot 4:13)

3. The ill tempered are not qualified to teach. (Pirkei Avot 2:6)

4. As you teach, you learn. (Midrash Psalms 11)

While sinning, repent (Ben Sirah 18:21)

Doing Teshuvah (Repentance)

1. Repent one day before your death. (Pirkei Avot 2:10)

2. Rend your hearts and not your garments. (Joel 2:13)

3. Always remember that the gates of repentance are open forever (Deuteronomy Rabbah 2:7)

4. Repentance that springs from love of God causes wilful sins to be treated as righteous deeds. (Talmud Yoma 86b)

5. Always do penitence while you still have your full strength. (Yalkut Shimoni to Ecclesiastes, 979)

There is a season and a time for every purpose under the heavens (Ecclesiastes 3:1)

Time

1. Whoever presses time is pressed by time. (Talmud Berachot 64)

2. Money is time, for every luxury costs so many precious hours of your life. (Chafetz Chayim)

3. How good is a word that is rightly timed. (Proverbs 15:23)

4. Time is short and flies away swifter than the shades of evening. (Jedaiah ben Bedersi)

One who honors the Torah is honored by all people (Pirkei Avot 4:6)

Torah

1. Where there is no Torah, there is no good conduct, and where there is no good conduct, there can be no Torah. (Pirkei Avot 3:17)

2. The only free person is one who engages in Torah study. (Pirkei Avot 6:2)

3. The more Torah, the more life. (Pirkei Avot 2:7)

4. The Torah is truth, and the purpose of knowing it is to live by it. (Maimonides)

Buy truth and do not sell it
(Proverbs 23:23)

Telling the Truth

1. Better is the truth even if it is bitter. (Mivchar Hapeninim)

2. The truth always rises to the top, like oil on water. (Osem Bosem)

3. It is not enough for a person to know the truth. One should also know the ways that leads to the knowledge of it. (Shapira)

4. A half truth is a whole lie. (Y. Tversky)

5. The seal of God is truth. (Talmud Shabbat 55a)

6. Teach your tongue to say, "I do not know," lest you be led to lie. (Talmud Berachot 4a)

Do not rejoice when your enemy falls in battle (Proverbs 24:17)

War

1. Common soldiers advance and start the battle but it is the experienced soldiers who go down into the fray and are victorious. (Talmud Berachot 53b)

2. A leader who doesn't suffer before he sends his nation into battle is not fit to be a leader. (Golda Meir)

3. When there is war in a land, there is neither justice nor law. (Abravenel)

4. Better overt war than covert peace. (S. Rubin)

If you wish to keep your affairs secret
drink no wine (Zohar iv, 177b)

Wine

1. Two things cannot go hand in hand: drinking wine and serving God prayerfully and with learning. (Zohar Chadash, i, 22b)

2. No good comes from wine. (Numbers Rabbah 10, 8)

3. Wine gladdens life. (Ecclesiastes 10:19)

4. Wine tops the list of all medicines. (Talmud Baba Batra 58)

5. A person should only sing over wine. (Talmud Berachot 35)

Wisdom is better than jewels
(Proverbs 8:11)

Becoming Wise

1. Study much and trade little. (Talmud Niddah 70)

2. Associate with wise people. (Proverbs 13:20)

3. Silence is a protective fence for wisdom. (Pirkei Avot: 3:13)

4. Try to learn from all people. (Pirkei Avot 4:1)

5. Try to be able to foresee what will transpire. (Talmud Tamid 32)

6. To acquire wisdom, study the way that money works. (Talmud Baba Batra 175b)

Whatever blessing dwells in the house comes from the wife (Talmud Baba Metzia 59a)

Wives and Husbands

1. One who loves his wife as himself and honors her more than himself, to him Scripture says "You shall know that your tent is in peace." (Talmud Yevamot 62b)

2. One who looks for the earnings of his wife never sees a sign of blessing. (Talmud Pesachim 50)

3. If your wife is of low stature, bend down to consult her. (Talmud Baba Metzia 59)

4. A man should eat less than he can afford, and should honor his wife and children more than he can afford. (Talmud Chullin 84)

5. If a husband and a wife are worthy, the Divine Presence abides among them. (Talmud Sotah 17)

If a person works, that person is blessed
(Midrash Psalm 23:3)

Work

1. Blessing only rests upon the work of one's hands. (Peskita Rabbati 19)

2. How lovely it is when Torah study is accompanied by worldly work. (Pirkei Avot 2:2)

3. A person should learn a trade, and God will send that person sustenance. (Ecclesiastes Rabbah 10:6)

4. A person can die if that person has nothing to do. (Avot de Rabbi Natan 11:23a)

The world is a tree and people its fruit
(Solomon ibn Gabirol)

The World

1. Just as your hand, held before the eye, can hide the tallest mountain, so this small earthly life keeps us from viewing the vast radiance that fills the core of the universe. (Nachman of Bratslav)

2. The world is new to us each morning. This is God's gift, and a person should believe that he is reborn each day. (Baal Shem Tov)

3. Each and every person should say: "The world was made for me." (Talmud Sanhedrin 37)

4. The entire world is a narrow bridge. The main thing is not to fear. (Nachman of Bratslav)

Praised are You, God, who revives the dead to life (Amidah)

The World to Come

1. The world is like a corridor leading to the world to come. Prepare yourself for the corridor, so that you may enter into the inner chamber. (Pirkei Avot, 4:21)

2. In the world to come, the righteous sit with their crowns on their heads and enjoy the radiance of the Divine Presence. (Talmud Berachot 17a)

3. Just people, whatever their nation, will be rewarded in the world to come. (Talmud Sanhedrin 105a)

4. Prepare yourself for this world as though you will live forever. Prepare yourself for the next world as though you will die tomorrow. (Shaashuim)